# Explore the Viking Age

Candice Ransom

Lerner Publications ◆ Minneapolis

Lerner Publications Company
An imprint of Lerner Publishing Group, Inc.
241 First Avenue North
Minneapolis, MN 55401 USA

For reading levels and more information, look up this title at www.lernerbooks.com.

Main body text set in Billy Infant Regular. Typeface provided by SparkyType.

**Editor:** Angel Kidd **Photo Editor:** Angel Kidd
**Lerner team:** Sue Marquis

**Library of Congress Cataloging-in-Publication Data**

Names: Ransom, Candice F., 1952- author
Title: Explore the Viking age / Candice Ransom.
Description: Minneapolis, MN : Lerner Publications, [2026] | Series: Lightning bolt books ®—early civilizations | Includes bibliographical references and index. | Audience: Ages 6-9 | Audience: Grades 2-3 | Summary: "To be a Viking was to live a life of sailing and raiding. Readers uncover experts' theories about why Vikings started raiding, where they were from, where they traveled to, and more"— Provided by publisher.
Identifiers: LCCN 2025011218 (print) | LCCN 2025011219 (ebook) | ISBN 9798765689295 library binding | ISBN 9798348028985 paperback | ISBN 9798765696866 epub
Subjects: LCSH: Vikings—Juvenile literature | Civilization, Viking—Juvenile literature
Classification: LCC DL66 .R36 2026 (print) | LCC DL66 (ebook) | DDC 948.022—dc23/eng/20250509

LC record available at https://lccn.loc.gov/2025011218
LC ebook record available at https://lccn.loc.gov/2025011219

Manufactured in the United States of America
1-1012506-54797-5/19/2025

# Table of Contents

# Who Were the Vikings?

The Vikings came from northern Europe. Their homelands were Norway, Sweden, and Denmark. They spoke a language called Old Norse.

The Vikings were not a civilization but a lifestyle. Their lands grew throughout the Viking Age.

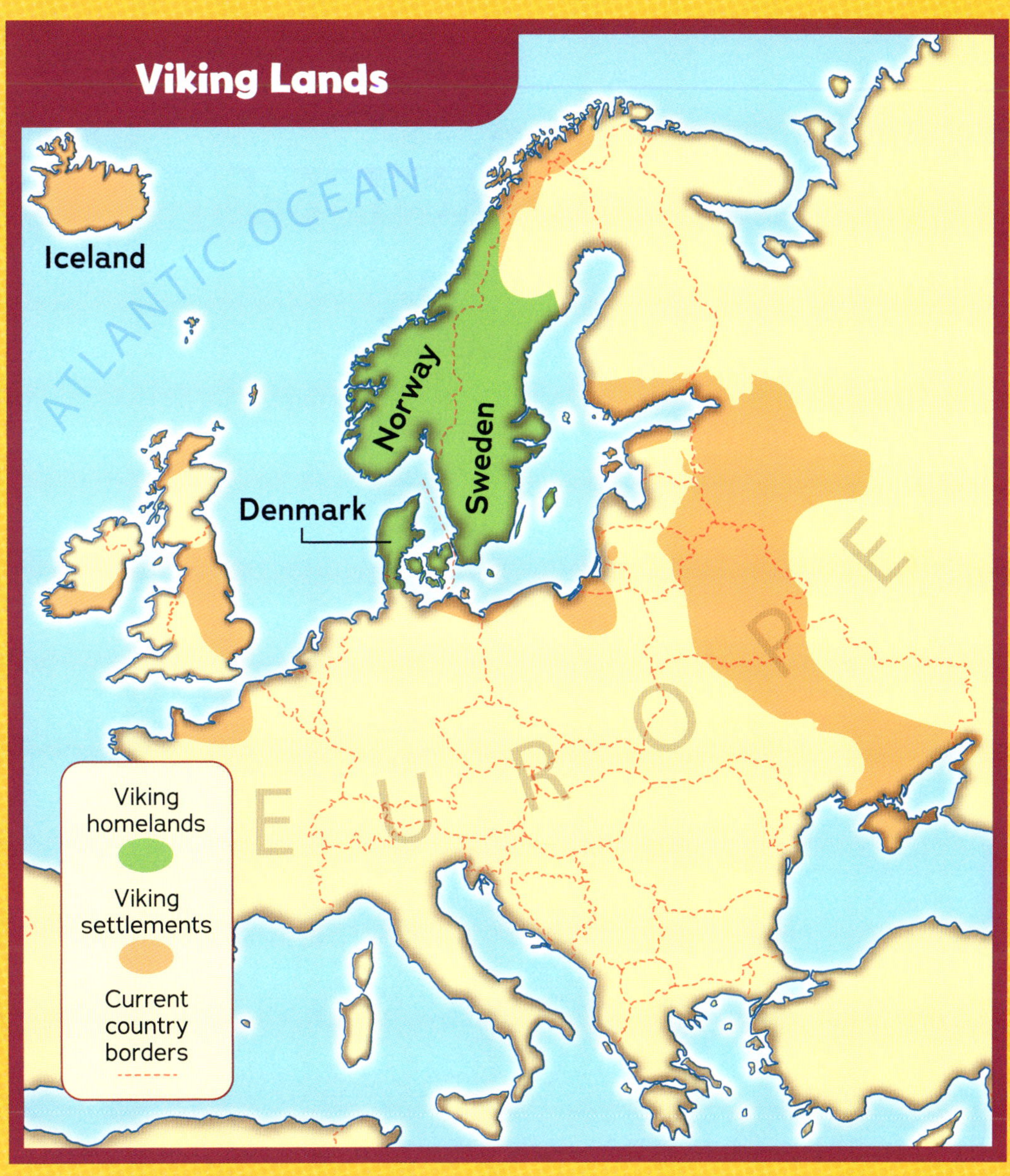

Wooden Viking boats were called longships.

In the late 700s, a group of Norsemen began sailing to other countries to steal from them. They raided churches and towns in England first.

Experts are not sure why Vikings went on raids. Some believe that their homeland could not grow enough food to feed them. It may have been easier to take from other countries.

Vikings used tricks to attack places such as Italy.

# Raiding and Trading

Europeans feared Viking sailors and their longships. Vikings fought with shields, swords, and axes to raid and take other people's lands.

A statue of Viking king Harald Fairhair in Norway

The Vikings settled in parts of England, Ireland, and Scotland. Viking kings ruled the people of these lands, made laws, and led Viking warriors.

Vikings sailed on rivers to attack France, Germany, and Spain. They sailed east to Russia, Turkey, and Iraq. **They traded furs and iron for spices and silk.**

Viking traders may have used tents like this one.

About 1,200 years ago, Vikings sailed across the Atlantic Ocean. They built settlements in Iceland and Greenland.

## Not all Vikings were raiders.

**Farmers grew barley and oats and raised sheep.**

A Viking farmhouse in Iceland

Metalworkers made jewelry and swords. Women wove cloth, and children helped with chores.

Vikings gave one another rings and bracelets.

The Vikings told long stories called sagas. These sagas were often about the many gods the Vikings worshipped. These included Odin and his sons Thor and Loki.

Odin had two ravens who gave him wisdom.

Vikings carved runes and pictures into large stones.

Vikings had their own alphabet. Letters called runes were carved on coins and stones.

# End of the Viking Age

When Vikings first began raiding other countries, the rulers in those lands were weak. The Vikings easily took over.

The Vikings failed to take over Paris, France.

Stronger leaders came to power in these countries. Their armies were trained to defend against Viking attacks. Rulers built forts to protect their lands.

During the Middle Ages, many people in Europe became Christians. Many Vikings also became Christians. Raiding and stealing was now against their religion.

In 1066, the last Viking king, Harald Hardrada, lost an important battle to the Duke of Normandy. After that, there were no more Viking raids. The Viking Age was over.

# Did the Vikings Land in North America?

One saga claims a Viking named Leif Eriksson sailed to a place he named Vinland. Other Vikings followed him to that part of what is now Newfoundland, Canada. In the 1960s, archaeologists dug up Viking items that were around a thousand years old. Experts believe this is proof Vikings landed in North America long before Christopher Columbus.

# Viking Age Facts

- Important Vikings who died were buried in their boats with their swords, jewelry, and even animals.
- Legend says the Viking god Thor made thunder with his hammer. The god Odin gave up an eye for wisdom.
- The Vikings discovered the country of Iceland. No people were living there until the Vikings arrived.

# Glossary

**age:** a time period

**civilization:** a large group of people who live in an area and share a common government and culture

**lifestyle:** way of life of a person or group

**longship:** a long sail and oar ship used by the Vikings

**Middle Ages:** a period in Europe from around 1,500 years ago to 500 years ago

**Norseman:** another word for Viking

**raider:** someone who attacks a place to steal from it

**religion:** a set of beliefs about how the universe was made and what its purpose is

**settlement:** a place people have recently moved to

## Learn More

Britannica Kids: Leif Eriksson
https://kids.britannica.com/kids/article/Leif-Eriksson/353374

Britannica Kids: Vikings
https://kids.britannica.com/kids/article/Vikings/353900

Conley, Kate A. *Loki.* Kids Core, 2024.

*National Geographic Kids*: 10 Facts about the Vikings
https://www.natgeokids.com/uk/discover/history/general-history/10-facts-about-the-vikings/

Stjern, Andy. *My Little Golden Book About Vikings.* Golden Books, 2024.

Wagner, Zelda. *Explore Ancient Greece.* Lerner Publications, 2026.

# Index



## Photo Acknowledgments

Image credits: clu/Getty Images, p. 4; Laura Westlund/Independent Picture Service, p. 5; maradon 333/Shutterstock, p. 6; Ivy Close Images/Getty Images, p. 7; WHPics/Alamy, p. 8; Christian Rueger/Shutterstock, p. 9; Stephen Roberts Photography/Alamy, p. 10; gorodenkoff/Getty Images, p. 11; Knut Hybinette/Alamy, p. 12; PRISMA ARCHIVO/Alamy, p. 13; Baloncici/Getty Images, p. 14; Mats O Andersson/Shutterstock, p. 15; powerofforever/Getty Images, p. 16; Print Collector/Getty Images, p. 17; Werner Forman/Getty Images, p. 18; Historical Images Archive/Alamy, p. 19; StephanHoerold/Getty Images, p. 20.

Cover: Maremagnum/Getty Images.